INVENTIONS AND DISCOVERY

MARIE ✲ CURIE
AND
RADIOACTIVITY

Connie Miller

illustrated by Scott Larson and Mark Heike

www.raintreepublishers.co.uk
Visit our website to find out
more information about
Raintree books.

Phone 0845 6044371
Fax +44 (0) 1865 312263
Email myorders@capstonepub.co.uk

Customers from outside the UK please telephone +44 1865 312262

Raintree is an imprint of Capstone Global Library Limited, a company incorporated in England and Wales
having its registered office at 7 Pilgrim Street, London, EC4V 6LB – Registered company number: 6695582

"Raintree" is a registered trademark of Pearson Education Limited, under licence to Capstone Global
Library Limited

Design: Alison Thiele and Ted Williams
UK editor: Diyan Leake
Originated by Capstone Global Library Ltd
Printed in China by South China Printing Company Ltd

ISBN 978 1 406 21571 7 (hardback)
14 13 12 11 10
10 9 8 7 6 5 4 3 2 1

British Library Cataloguing in Publication Data
Miller, Connie -- Marie Curie and radioactivity
A full catalogue record for this book is available from the British Library.

Every effort has been made to contact copyright holders of material reproduced in this book. Any omissions
will be rectified in subsequent printings if notice is given to the publisher.

Disclaimer
All the Internet addresses (URLs) given in this book were valid at the time of going to press. However, due to
the dynamic nature of the Internet, some addresses may have changed, or sites may have changed or ceased
to exist since publication. While the author and publisher regret any inconvenience this may cause readers, no
responsibility for any such changes can be accepted by either the author or the publisher.

Editor's note: Direct quotations from primary sources are indicated by a yellow background.

Direct quotations appear on the following pages:
Page 17, from Marie Curie's letter to Joseph Sklodèovski, 11 December 1903, as printed in
Eve Curie's *Madame Curie: A Biography* (Garden City, N.Y.: Doubleday, Doran and
Company, Inc., 1938).
Page 18, from Pierre Curie's letter to George Gouy, 7 November 1905, as printed in Eve
Curie's *Madame Curie: A Biography* (Garden City, N.Y.: Doubleday, Doran and Company,
Inc., 1938).
Page 22, from Marie Curie's letter to Bronya Dluska, 10 November 1920, as printed in
Eve Curie's *Madame Curie: A Biography* (Garden City, N.Y.: Doubleday, Doran and
Company, Inc., 1938).

CONTENTS

CHAPTER 1
THE CURIES

In 1897, Marie Curie and her husband Pierre lived in Paris, France. Marie had moved to Paris from Poland in 1891 to study physics and math at the Sorbonne. At the time, the Sorbonne was the only university in Europe that allowed women to attend. Pierre ran the laboratory at the Municipal School of Industrial Physics and Chemistry.

Marie, it's time to go home. Irène needs her parents, and we need our sleep.

I have just one more note to make.

CHAPTER 2

THE DISCOVERY

Pitchblende was considered mine waste after the uranium was removed. Mine owners were happy to give it to the Curies for their experiments. Only a very small amount of uranium remained in the pitchblende.

Look at these readings, Pierre. I expected the pitchblende to give out less energy than pure uranium. But it has more.

There must be some mistake. Let's test it again.

I have already retested it.

This can only mean one thing.

A new element is giving off all that energy!

Isolating the radium was difficult work. Finally, on 28 March 1902, Marie and Pierre Curie isolated a pure sample of radium.

After four years we've finally done it!

It is beautiful!

Congratulations!

At the time, no one knew that radiation gives off so much energy that it damages the body. The Curies did not know that the radium was making them ill.

My bones ache, Marie. My fingers and legs are especially sore.

You need rest, Pierre. We have been working too hard. Let's take a holiday to the countryside.

A few months later, Marie wrote the final paper for her degree. She was awarded the title of Doctor of Physical Sciences. She finished with high honours.

Chapter 3
Radium and Radiation Therapy

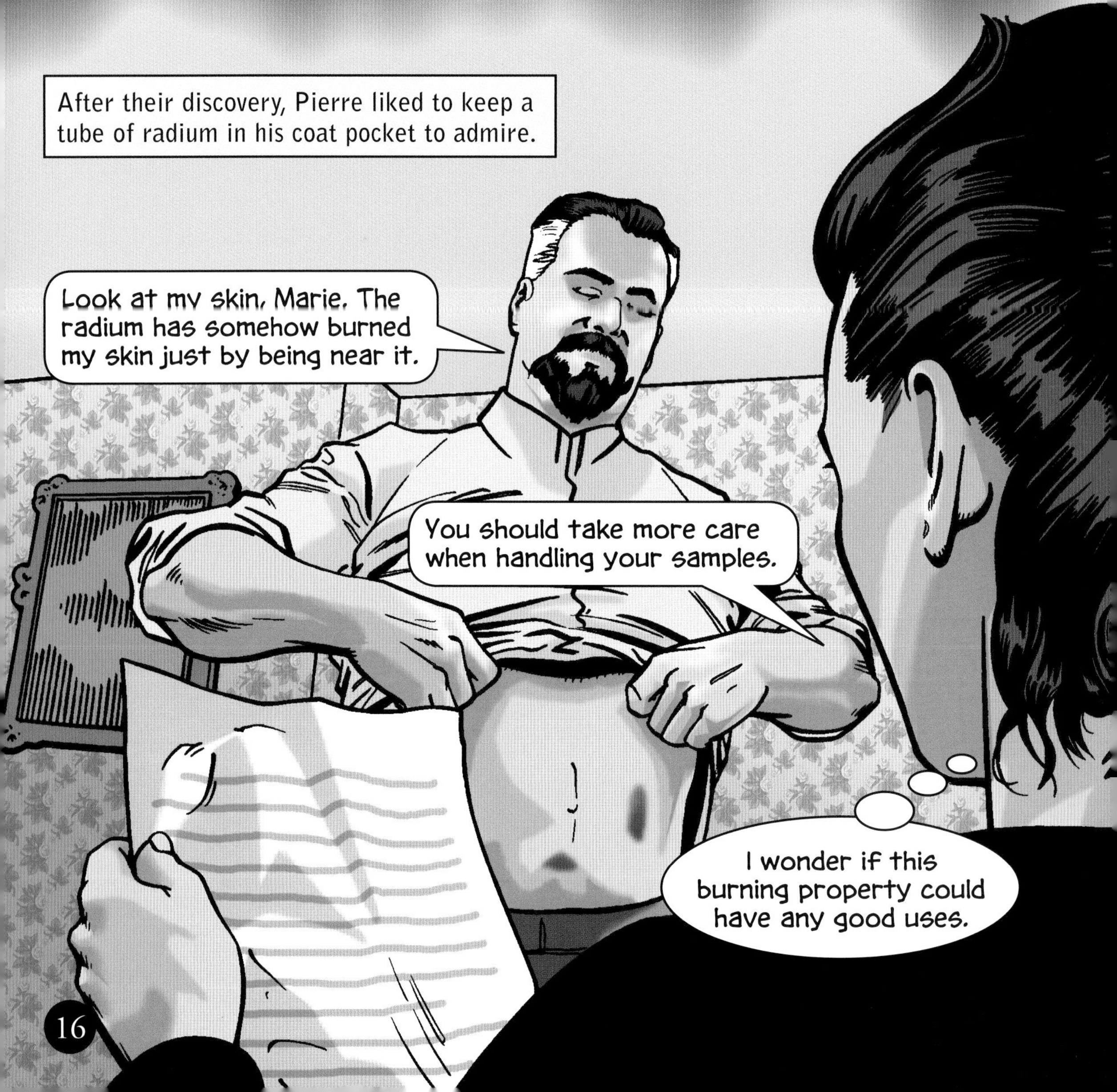

In 1904, Marie gave birth to a second daughter, Eve. Marie continued to work in the lab and at home. But Pierre was becoming even more ill.

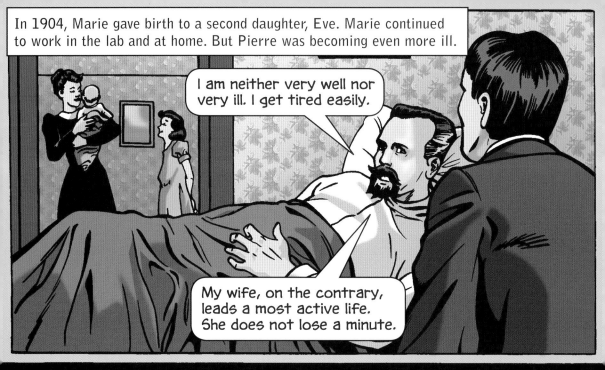

I am neither very well nor very ill. I get tired easily.

My wife, on the contrary, leads a most active life. She does not lose a minute.

Only two years later, Pierre was struck by a horse-drawn wagon and killed. He was 47 years old.

Good-bye, Pierre. Your coffin is closed and I can see you no more.

CHAPTER 4

THE CURIE LEGACY

My greatest troubles come from my eyes and ears. My eyes have grown much weaker. As for the ears, an almost continuous humming, sometimes very intense, persecutes me.

Marie, you need to rest. You aren't a young woman anymore. Let your daughters pick up your work where you left off.

It is my work that keeps me going, dear friend!

Over the next 10 years, Marie became more sick and weak. Still, she worked in her lab, advised her students, and went about raising money for her work.

Irène Curie and her husband Frédéric Joliot continued to study where Marie left off.

In 1935, Irène and Frédéric earned the Nobel Prize in Chemistry for their discovery of artificial radioactivity.

Your mother would have been so proud!

At least we were able to show her our discovery before she died. It was her last great pleasure.

MORE ABOUT
MARIE ⚛ CURIE
AND
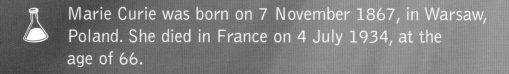
RADIOACTIVITY

Marie Curie was born on 7 November 1867, in Warsaw, Poland. She died in France on 4 July 1934, at the age of 66.

Marie invented the term *radioactivity* to describe the energy given off by polonium and radium.

Marie took notes in her laboratory notebooks while doing research on radium. As a result, the radiation that harmed her body also got into her notebooks. Even today, Marie's notebooks are too radioactive to handle safely.

After the Curies discovered radium, many companies wanted to use it in their products. Marie and Pierre could have made money by patenting their process for collecting radium. Instead, they believed radium belonged to everyone. They felt other scientists should be allowed to find ways for radium to benefit the world.

Marie is the only person ever awarded two Nobel Science Prizes in different subjects. She won the Nobel Prize in Physics in 1903. Her 1911 Nobel Prize was in chemistry.

Marie's mobile X-ray vehicles were nicknamed *petites Curies,* or "little Curies". By the end of World War I (1914–1918), Marie's fleet of 20 *petites Curies* had helped more than 1 million soldiers.

 Marie and Pierre studied ways radioactivity could be used in medicine to help people. But the discovery of radioactivity also had a negative side. It led to the creation of the atomic bombs the United States dropped on Japan near the end of World War II (1939–1945).

 In 1995, Marie's and Pierre's remains were moved from their original burial site in Sceaux, France. They were reburied in a place of honour under the dome of the Panthéon in Paris.

GLOSSARY

element basic substance in chemistry that cannot be split into simpler substances

persecute cause to suffer

physics the study of matter and energy, including light, heat, electricity, and motion

radiation tiny particles sent out from radioactive material

radioactivity a process in which atoms break apart and create a lot of energy

uranium a silver-white radioactive metal that is the main source of nuclear energy

INTERNET SITES

http://www.mariecurie.org.uk/aboutus/MarieCuriethescientist/

This page provides a brief profile of Marie Curie, the inspiration behind the founding of the Marie Curie Cancer Care charity.

http://www.mariecurie.co.uk/

This website lists key dates in Marie Curie's life and provides quotes from and about her.

MORE BOOKS TO READ

Curie and the Science of Radioactivity, Ian Graham (Barron's Educational Series, 2006)

Marie Curie (Great Lives series), Philip Steele (QED Publishing, 2007)

Marie Curie, Kathleen Krull (Viking, 2007)

Marie Curie, Vicki Cobb (Dorling Kindersley, 2008)

Marie Curie: Mother of Modern Physics, Janice Borzendowski (Sterling, 2009)

The Search for Radium: Marie Curie's Story, C. Birmingham (Mathew Price Ltd, 2006)

FIND OUT MORE

Marie Curie's office and personal chemistry laboratory have been preserved at the Curie Museum in the Institute Curie.
26 rue d'Ulm
75248 Paris cedex 05
France
Telephone +33 (0)1 56 24 55 00
http://www.curie.fr/fondation/musee/index.cfm/lang/_gb.htm

Visit the tomb where Marie Curie's ashes are buried and where she was the first woman to be so honoured.
Place du Panthéon
75005 Paris
France
http://www.pantheonparis.com/

INDEX